The Mirror
Puzzle Book

Glue these mirrors
to the mirror
stands which you
will find at the
back of the book.

TARQUIN PUBLICATIONS

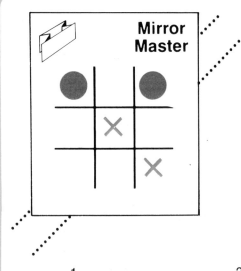

Trial and Error

The natural way to start is to use trial and error methods. Use this '**Mirror Master**' as an example and place the mirror on it. Slowly move the mirror about and see how the image changes. After a few minutes you will be able to find at least one of the patterns below. If not, there are some lines to help !

When you find design 1 on the '**Mirror Master**' it looks exactly the same as the drawing you are trying to match. It lies in the same direction on the page. Designs 2 and 3 can also be found on the '**Mirror Master**' but their solutions do not lie in the same direction on the page. This does not matter. It is the shape, size and colour which has to match, not the position on the page.

1

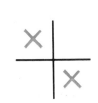

2

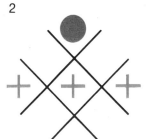

3

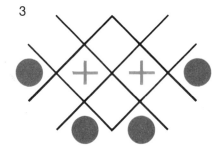

Logical Thinking

After you have solved some mirror puzzles by trial and error, you will begin to understand how to place the mirror in the right position straight away. In this example, how can you make the red dots disappear? How can you make one red dot and not two? How can you make an odd number of green crosses? See if you can work out what you have to do.

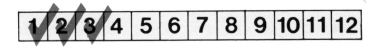

Mark off each puzzle as you solve it. Then you will be able to concentrate on the harder ones.

The Chart of Impossibility

After a while you may find that there are some puzzles you simply cannot solve. Don't despair. On every page there are some which are really impossible. No-one can do them !

To understand why certain shapes cannot be done is just as interesting and important as finding those which can.

On this chart the blue squares show which shapes are possible and the red squares which are impossible.

But before you can check your answers you have to work out which row belongs to which mirror puzzle. The rows are not in alphabetical order !

Write the letters A to L of the Mirror Puzzles in the empty grey squares when you have worked out which goes where.

Do it in pencil because you might not be right first time !

	1	2	3	4	5	6	7	8	9	10	11	12

Two can play

At the back of the book is another set of '**Mirror Masters**'. Cut the page out and then you and a friend can both puzzle at the same time.

Very young children who find it difficult to match designs which are not parallel can turn this special page round until two images face the same way.

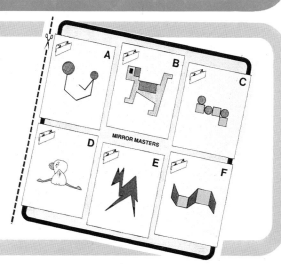

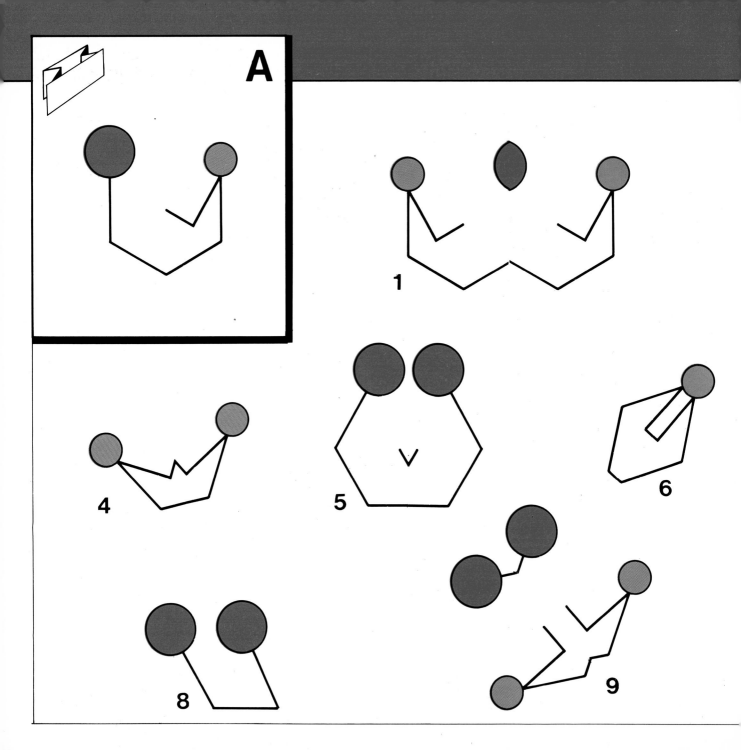

A

1

4

5

6

8

9

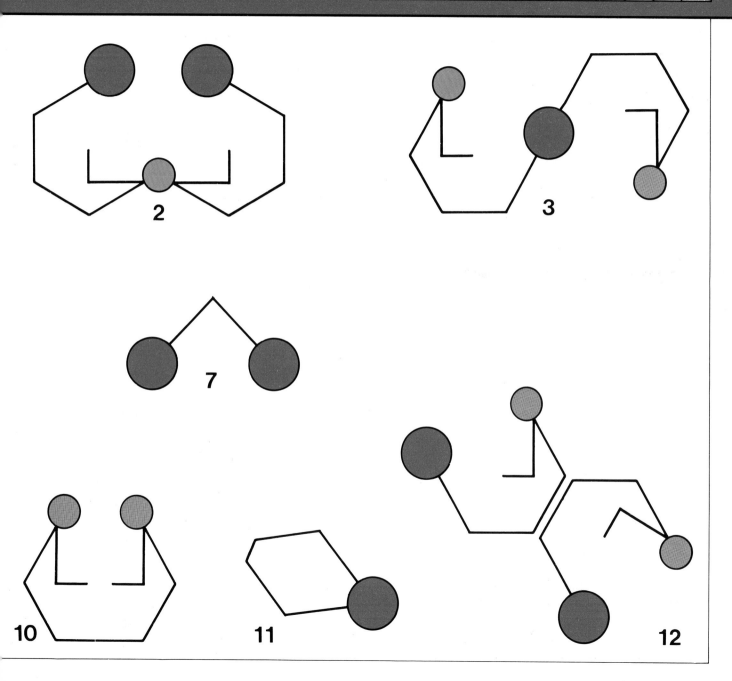

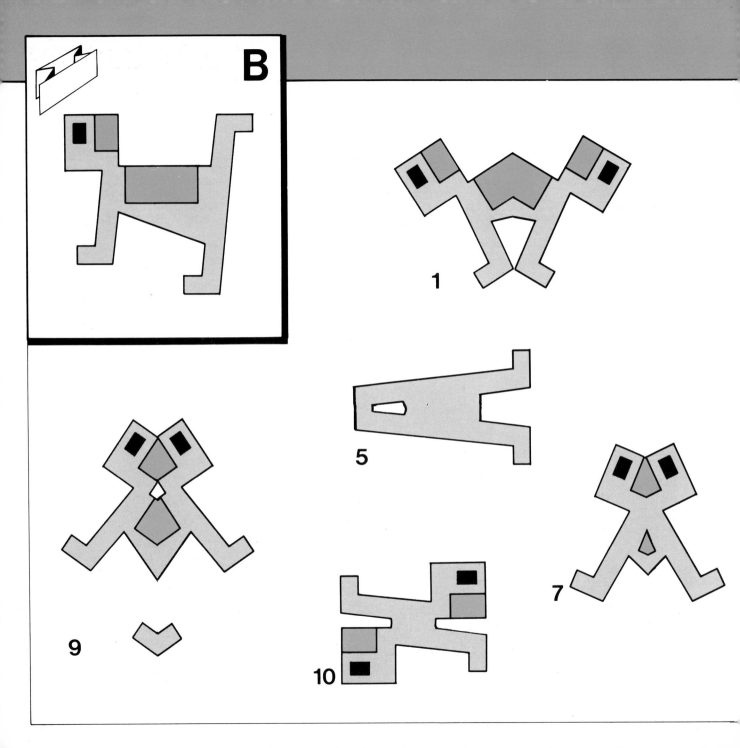

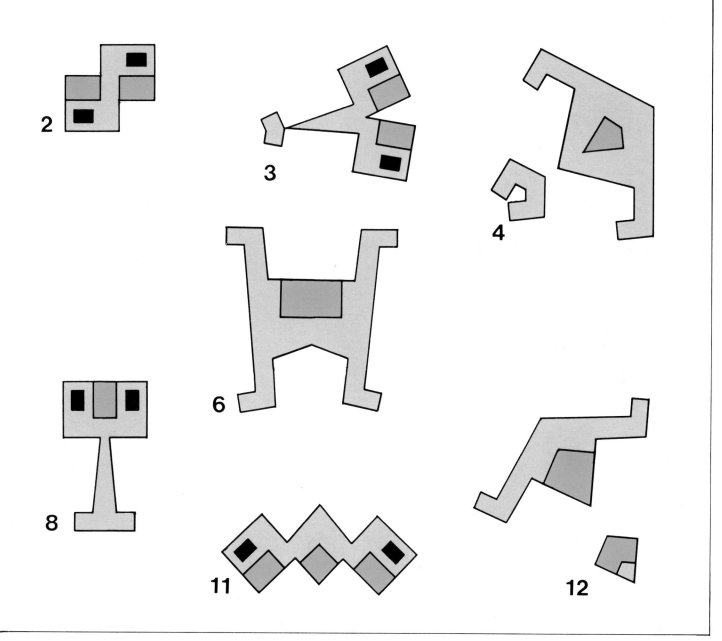

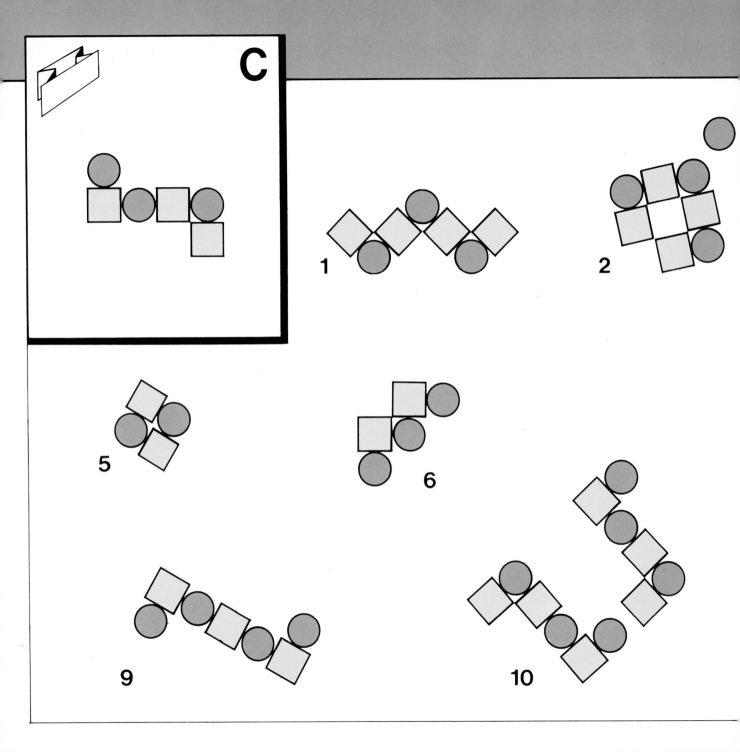

C

1

2

5

6

9

10

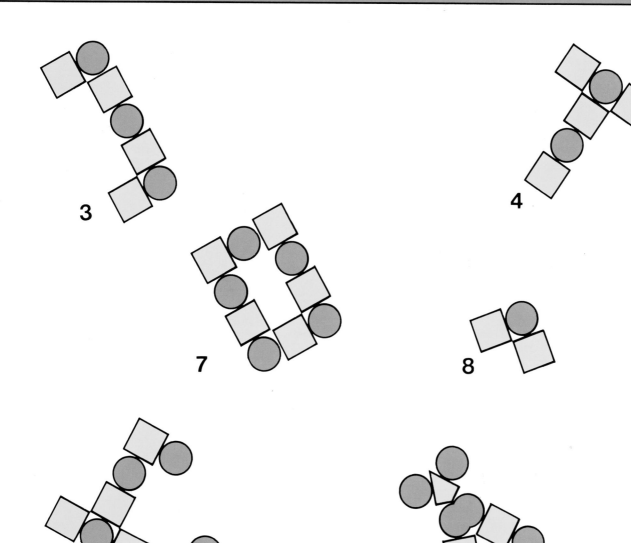

3

4

7

8

11

12

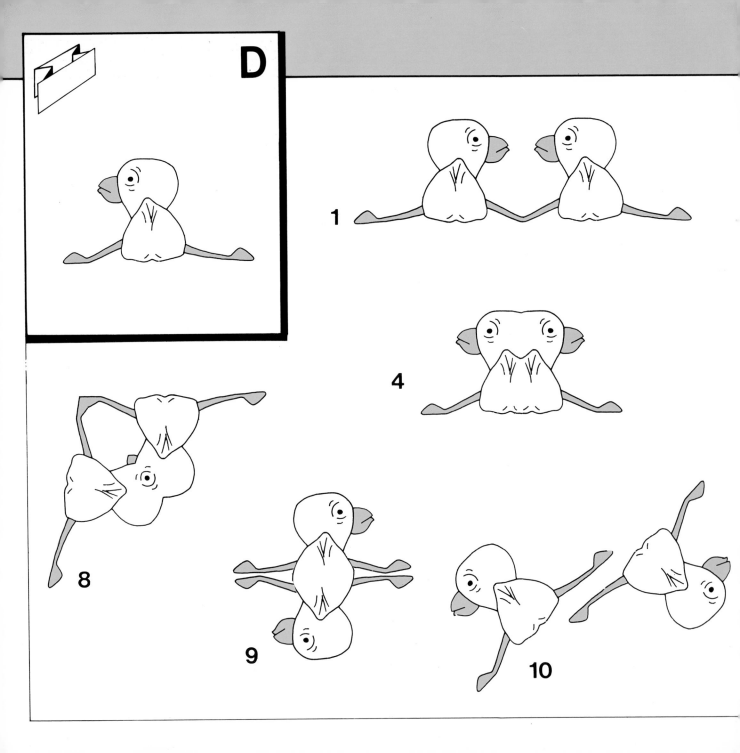

D

1

4

8

9

10

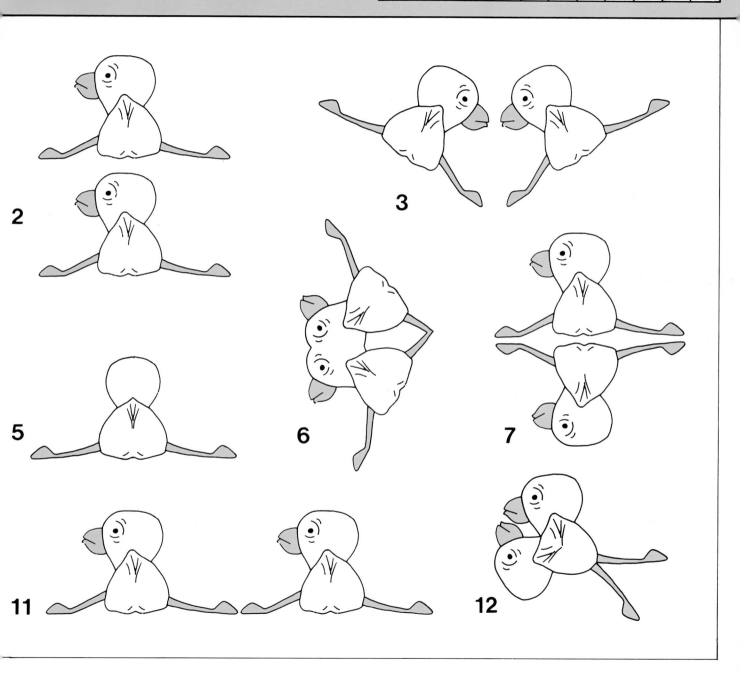

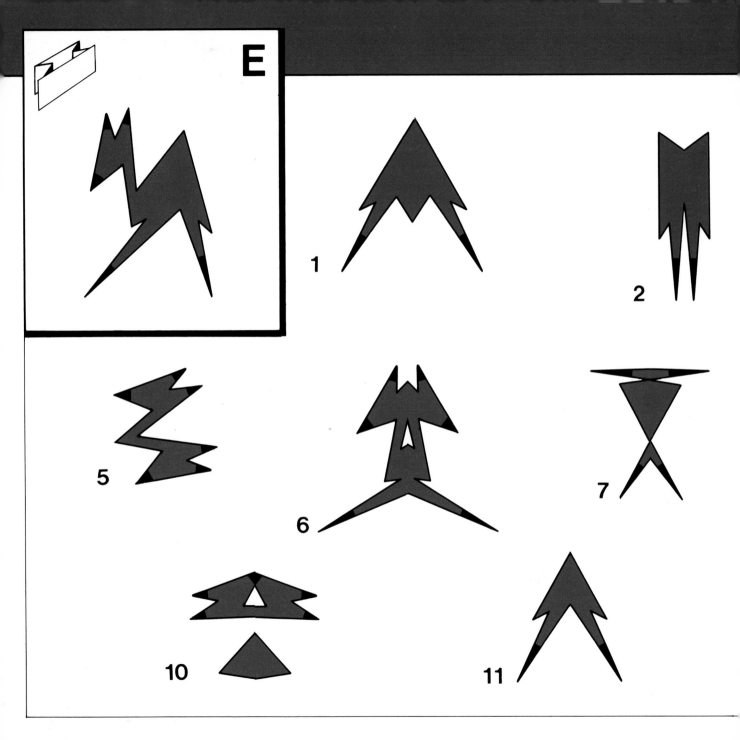

E

1

2

5

6

7

10

11

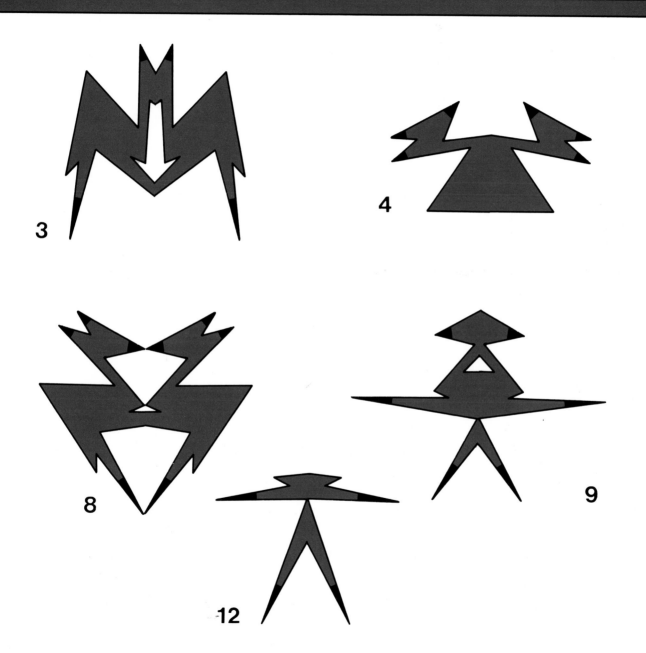

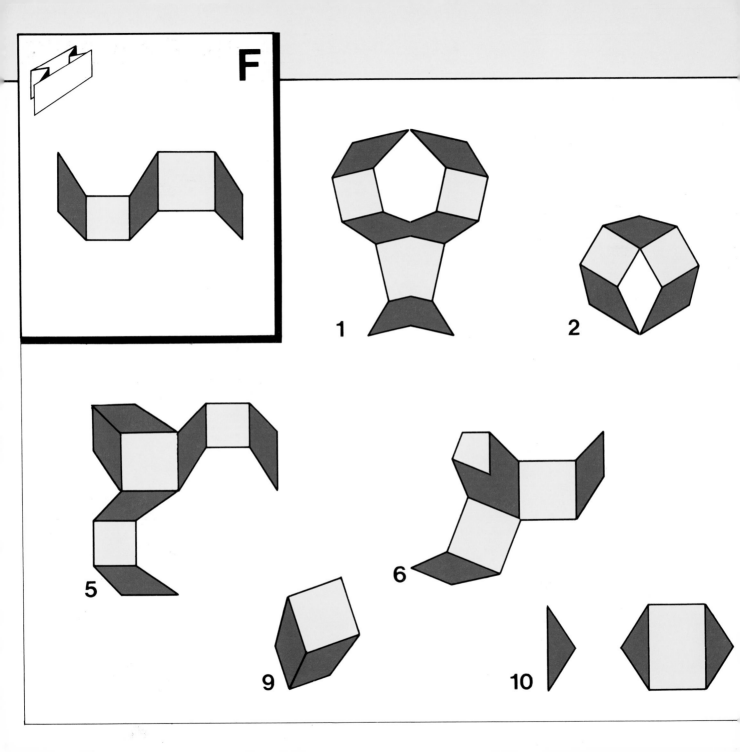

F

1

2

5

6

9

10

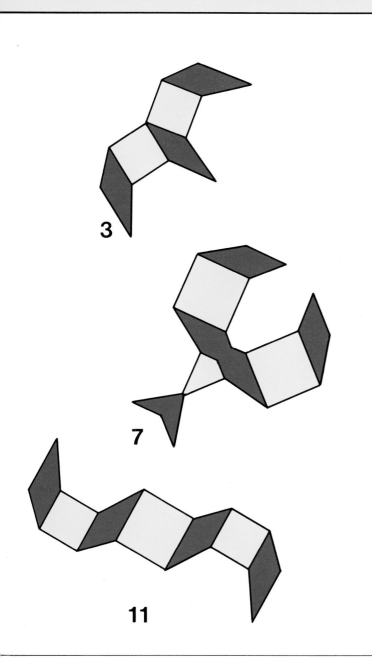

3

7

11

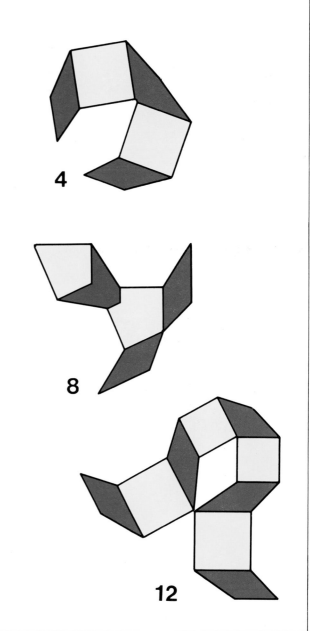

4

8

12

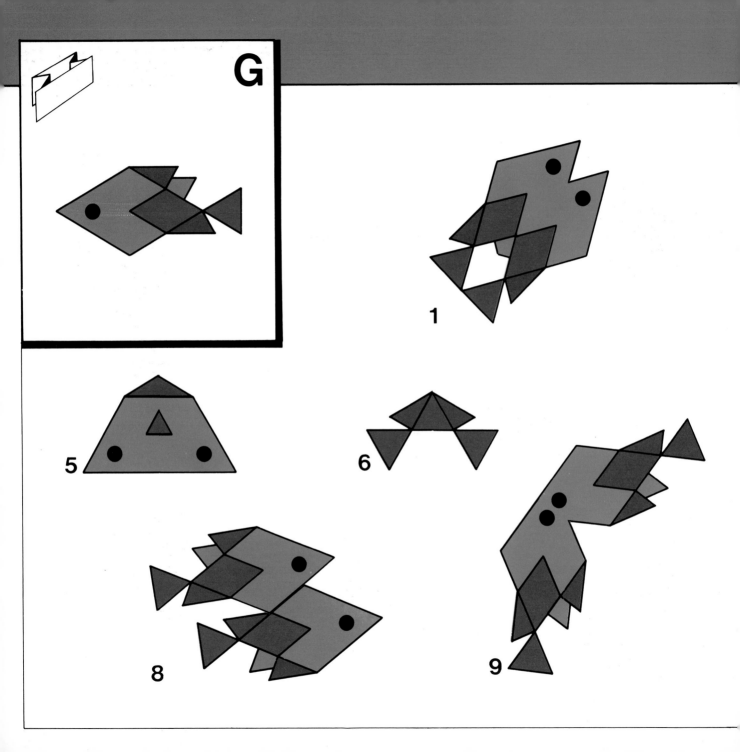

G

1

5

6

8

9

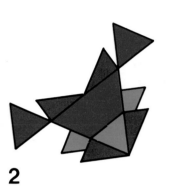

2

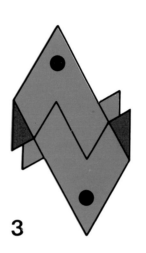

3

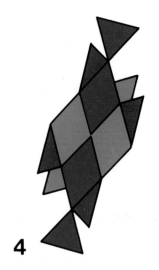

4

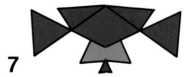

7

12

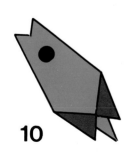

10

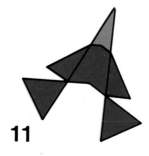

11

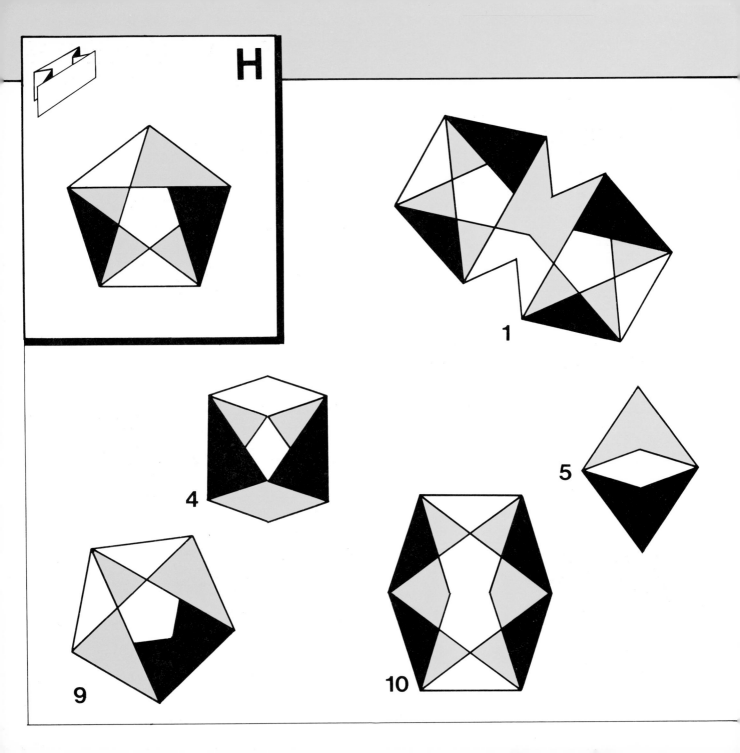

H

1

4

5

9

10

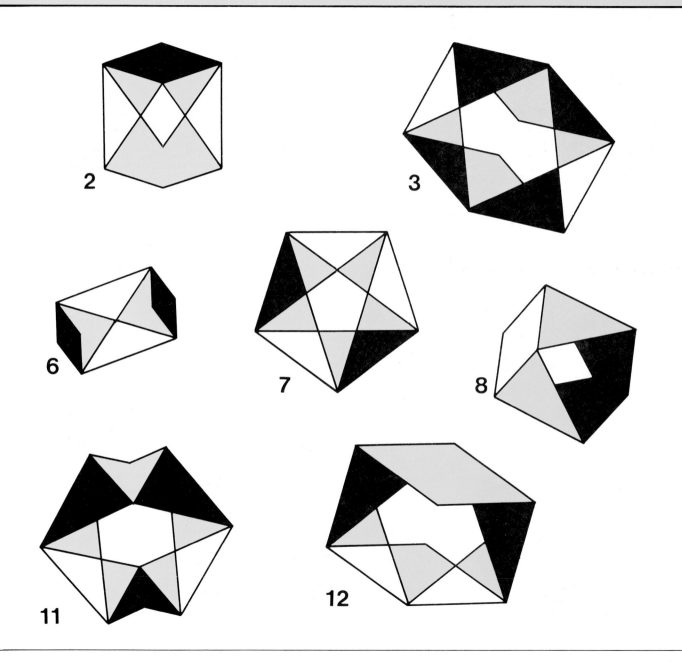

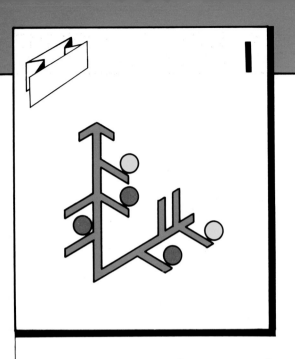

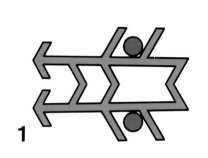

1

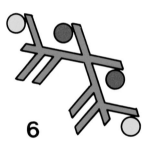

2

6

5

8

9

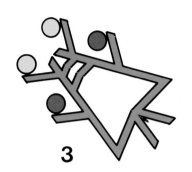

3

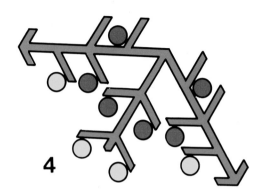

4

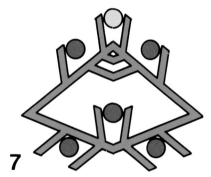

7

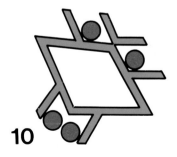

10

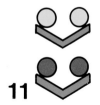

11

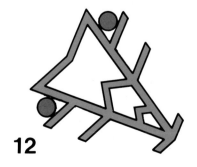

12

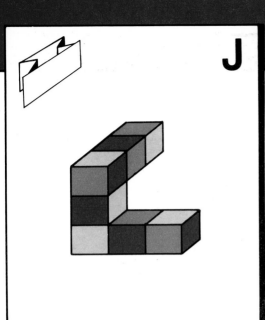

J

1

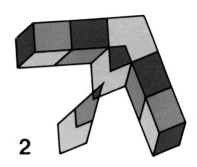

2

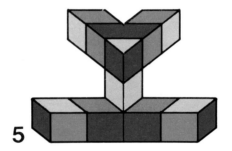

5

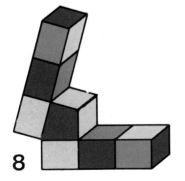

8

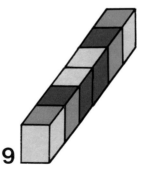

9

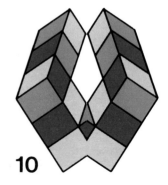

10

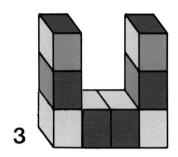

3

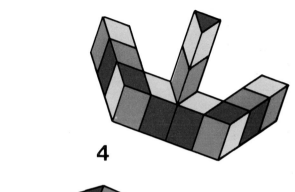

4

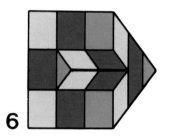

6

7

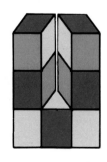

11

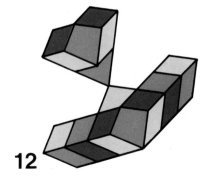

12

K

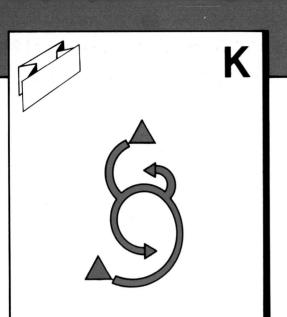

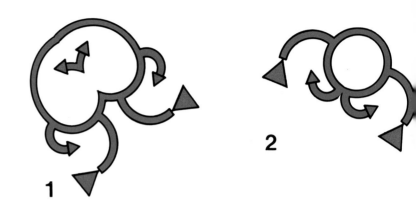

1

2

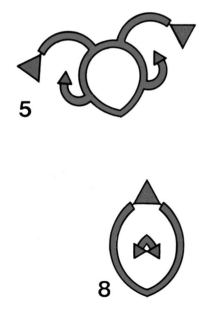

5

6

8

9

3

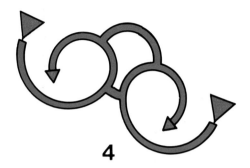

4

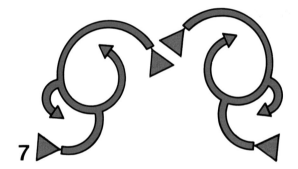

7

10

11

12

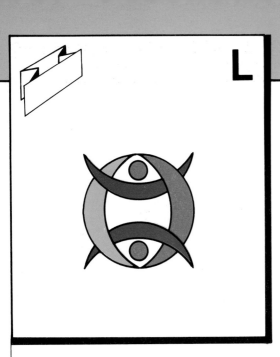

L

1

2

5

6

9

10

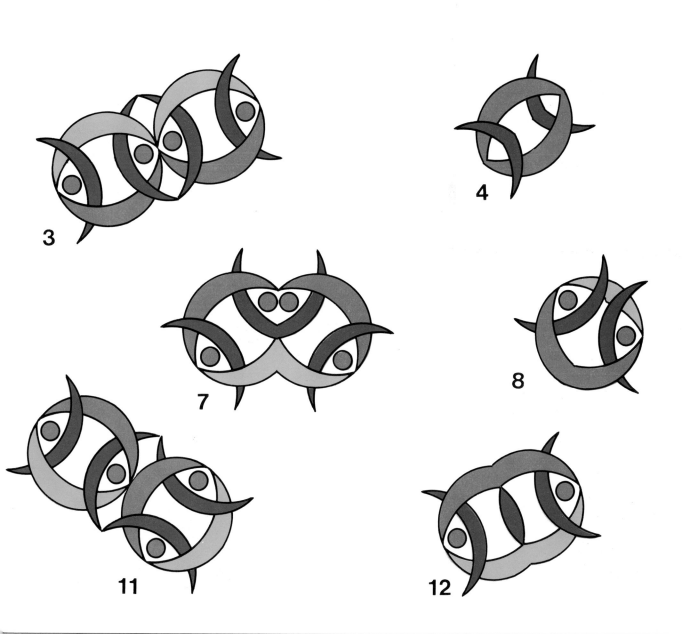

Symmetry, just symmetry . . .

Did you notice as you tried the puzzles that every pattern that was possible to make had a line of symmetry?

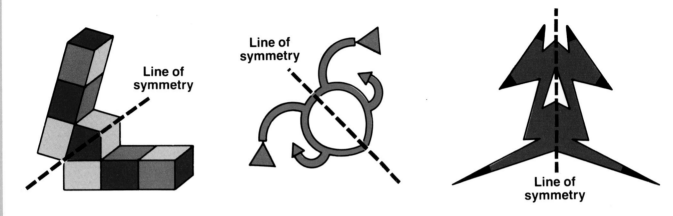

If you place the mirror on a line of symmetry, then the pattern you see is exactly the same whether the mirror is there or not. In other positions you see changes. Try it on these three patterns. Every time that you placed the mirror on the '**Mirror Master**' it created a pattern which had a line of symmetry along the mirror. Did you find any patterns that had a line of symmetry but which could not be made from the '**Mirror Master**'? Can you say why?

Some shapes have more than one line of symmetry. Some have none.

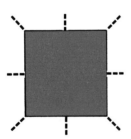

A square has four lines of symmetry. Place the mirror on each of the four lines and see how the square is unchanged. Can you place the mirror to make squares of different sizes?

Any line which passes through the centre of a circle is a line of symmetry but can you place the mirror to make different sized circles?

Symmetry is a fascinating subject and it is hoped that you will use your mirrors to do other experiments and to create some new puzzles of your own. Apart from that, you could tape the two mirrors together and experiment with different angles between them. But that is another story . . .

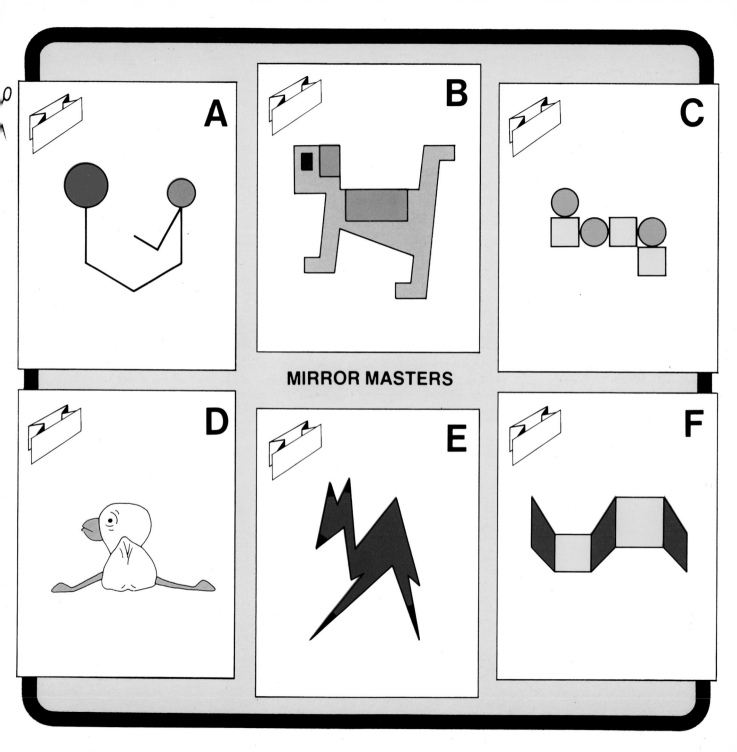

MIRROR MASTERS

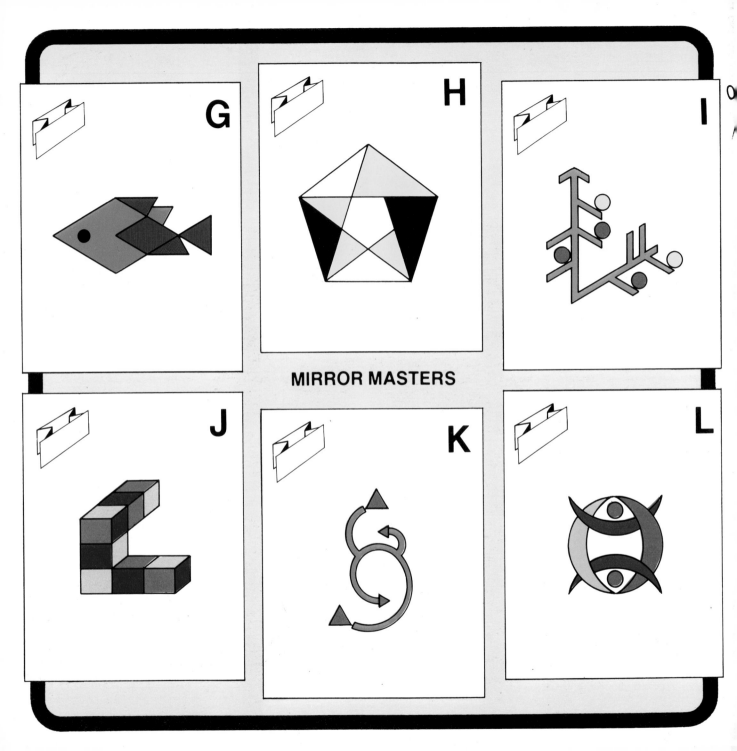

G

H

I

MIRROR MASTERS

J

K

L

Two Mirror Stands

1. Remove this page from the book.
2. Score along all lines marked. ▶◀
3. Crease firmly along the fold lines and then glue frame together using flaps A and B and the other using flaps C and D.
4. Glue the backs of each mirror to the stand.

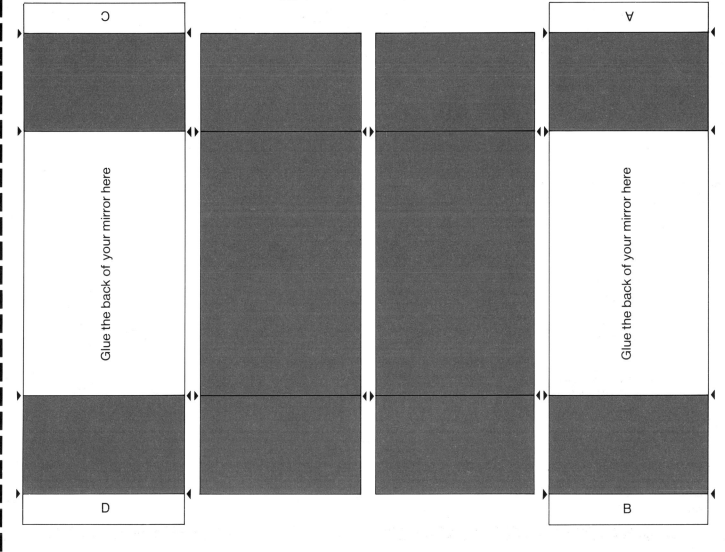

C

Glue the back of your mirror here

D

A

Glue the back of your mirror here

B

A   C

B   D